He That Dwelleth in the Secret Place of the Most High

For Unaccompanied Choir (SSAATTBB) with Soloists (S.

Psalm 91

*The soloists to stand with the chorus and not separately.

say of the Lord,_____ He is my re-fuge and my for-tress; My God,_____ in whom I trust. For he shall de-

say of the Lord,_____ He is my re-fuge and my for-tress; My God,_____ in whom I trust. For he shall de-

say of the Lord,_____ He is my re-fuge and my for-tress; My God,_____ in whom I trust. For he shall de-

say_____ of the Lord,_____ He is my re-fuge and my for-tress; My God,_____ in whom I trust. For he shall de-

li-ver me from the snare of the fow-ler, and from the noi-some pes-ti-lence. He shall co-ver thee with his

li-ver me from the snare of the fow-ler, and from the noi-some pes-ti-lence. He shall co-ver thee with his

li-ver me from the snare of the fow-ler, and from the noi-some pes-ti-lence. He shall co-ver

li-ver me from the snare of the fow-ler, and from the noi-some pes-ti-lence. He shall co-ver thee with_____

18
pin - ions, and un - der his wings shalt thou take re - fuge: His
pin - ions, and un - der his wings shalt thou take re - fuge: His
pin - ions, and un - - der his wings shalt thou take re - fuge: His
pin - ions, and un - - der his wings shalt thou take re - fuge: His
thee with his pin-ions, and un - der his wings shalt thou take
thee with his pin-ions, and un - - der his wings shalt thou take re - fuge:
his pin - nions, and un - der his wings shalt thou take
his pin - nions, and un - der his wings shalt thou take
3
f

21
S. 1
truth is a shield and a
S. 2
truth is a shield and a
A. 1
truth is a shield, his truth is a shield and a
A. 2
truth is a shield, his truth is a shield, is a shield and a
T. 1
re - fuge: His truth is a shield, is a shield and a
T. 2
His truth his truth is a shield, is a shield and a
B. 1
re - fuge: His truth is a shield, his truth is a shield and a
B. 2
re - fuge: His truth is a shield and a

24
Poco più mosso
Thou shalt not be a-fraid for the ter-ror by night;
Nor for the ar-row that fli-eth by day;
Nor for the
Poco più mosso
sfp unis. pp
pp sempre
buck - ler. His truth is a
Poco più mosso
sfp pp pp sempre

27

Nor — for the de - struc-tion   that wast-eth at   noon - day.

Nor — for the de - struc-tion   that wast-eth at   noon - day.

pes - ti-lence that walk-eth in   dark - ness;

shield_____ and a   buck - ler._____ A

shield_____ and a   buck - - - ler. A

shield_____ and a   buck - - - ler. A

shield_____ and a   buck - ler._____ A thou-sand shall

31

thou - sand shall fall at thy side, and ten thou - sand at thy right hand; But

thou - sand shall fall at thy side, and ten thou - sand at thy right hand; But

thou - sand shall fall at thy side, and ten thou - sand at thy right hand;

fall,_____ and ten_____ thou - sand at thy right hand;

34

Poco più lento

it_____ shall not come near thee.

it_____ shall not come near thee. But it

it shall not come near thee.

On - ly with thine eyes_____ shalt thou be -

37
For
morendo
ppp
tutti
shall not come near thee.
For
For thou, for
p
hold, and see the re - ward of the wick - ed.
For
morendo
p
40
mf espr.
thou, O Lord, art my re - fuge! Thou hast made the Most High thy ha - bi -
mf espr.
thou, O Lord, art my re - fuge! Thou hast made the Most
mf espr.
1
thou, O Lord, art my re - fuge! Thou hast made the
T.
mf espr.
2
thou, O Lord, art my re - fuge! Thou hast made the Most
mf espr.
thou, O Lord, art my re - fuge! Thou hast made the Most
mf espr.

43
mf
ta - tion; There shall no e - vil be - fall thee,
mf There shall no e - vil be - fall thee,
High thy ha - bi - ta - tion;
There shall no e - vil be - fall thee,
mf
Most High thy ha - bi - ta - tion; Then shall no e - vil be -
mf
High thy ha - bi - ta - tion; There shall no e - vil be -
mf
High thy ha - bi - ta - tion; There shall no e - vil be -
mf
46
dim. p molto cresc. f
nei-ther shall a - ny plague come nigh thy dwell - ing. For he shall give his an - gels
nei-ther shall a - ny plague come nigh thy dwell - ing. For he shall give his an - gels
fall thee, nei-ther shall a - ny plague come nigh thy dwell-ing. For he shall give his
fall thee, nei-ther shall a - ny plague come nigh thy dwell-ing. For he shall give his
fall thee, nei - ther shall a - ny plague come nigh thy dwell - ing. For he shall
dim.
p
molto cresc.
f

49 charge o-ver thee, to keep thee in all thy ways. They shall

charge o-ver thee, to keep thee in all thy ways. They shall

an-gels charge o-ver thee, to keep thee in

an-gels charge o-ver thee, to keep thee in all thy ways.

give his an-gels charge o-ver thee, to keep thee in all thy

52 bear thee up in their hands, lest thou dash thy foot a-gainst a

bear thee up in their hands, lest thou dash thy foot a-gainst a

They shall bear thee up in their hands, lest thou dash thy foot a-gainst a

all thy ways. They shall bear thee up in their hands, lest thou

They shall bear thee up in their hands, lest thou dash thy

ways. They shall bear thee up in their hands, lest thou dash thy foot

55
Più animato
stone.
stone.
mf
stone. Thou shalt tread up - on the li - on and ad - der: the young
mf marc.
stone. Thou shalt tread up - on the li - on and the
dash thy foot a - gainst a stone. The young
mf marc.
foot a - gainst a stone. Thou shalt tread up - on the li - on and the
B.
a - gainst a stone. Thou shalt tread up - on the li - on and the
Più animato
mf

58
f appassionato
S. 1
Be - cause he hath set his love up -
S. 2
Be - cause he hath set his love up -
A. 1
li - on and the ser - pent shalt thou tram - ple un - der feet. He hath set his
A. 2
ser - pent shalt thou tram-ple un-der feet. Be - cause he hath set his
T. 1
li - on and the ser - pent shalt thou tram - ple un - der feet. Be - cause he hath set his
T. 2
ser - pent shalt thou tram - ple un - der feet. He hath set his
B.
ser - pent shalt thou tram - ple un - der feet. Be - cause he
f

Più lento

on me, ___ there - fore will I de - li - ver him: I will set ___

on me, ___ there - fore will I de - li - ver him: I will set him on

love up - on me there - fore will I de - li - ver him: ___ I will

___ love up - on me, there - fore ___ will I ___ de - li - ver him: I will set ___

___ love up - on me, there - fore ___ will I ___ de - li - ver him: I will set ___

love up - on me, there - fore will I de - li - ver him: ___ I will

hath set his love up - on me, I will

him ___ on high, ___ be - cause he hath known my

high, I will set him on high, ___ be - cause ___ he hath known my

set him, I will set ___ him on high, be - cause ___ he hath known my

him ___ on high, ___ be - cause he hath known my

___ him on high, ___ I will set ___ him on high, be - cause ___ he ___ hath known my

set him, I will set ___ him on high, be - cause ___ he ___ hath known my

set him on high, be - cause he hath known my

71
Tempo I
f
mf
poco
He shall call up - on me, and I will an - swer
fff
ppp sempre
ppp
name. He shall call up - on me, and I will
name. He shall call up - on me, and I will
name. He shall call up - on me, and I will
name. He shall call up - on me, and I will
Tempo I
fff
ppp sempre
ppp

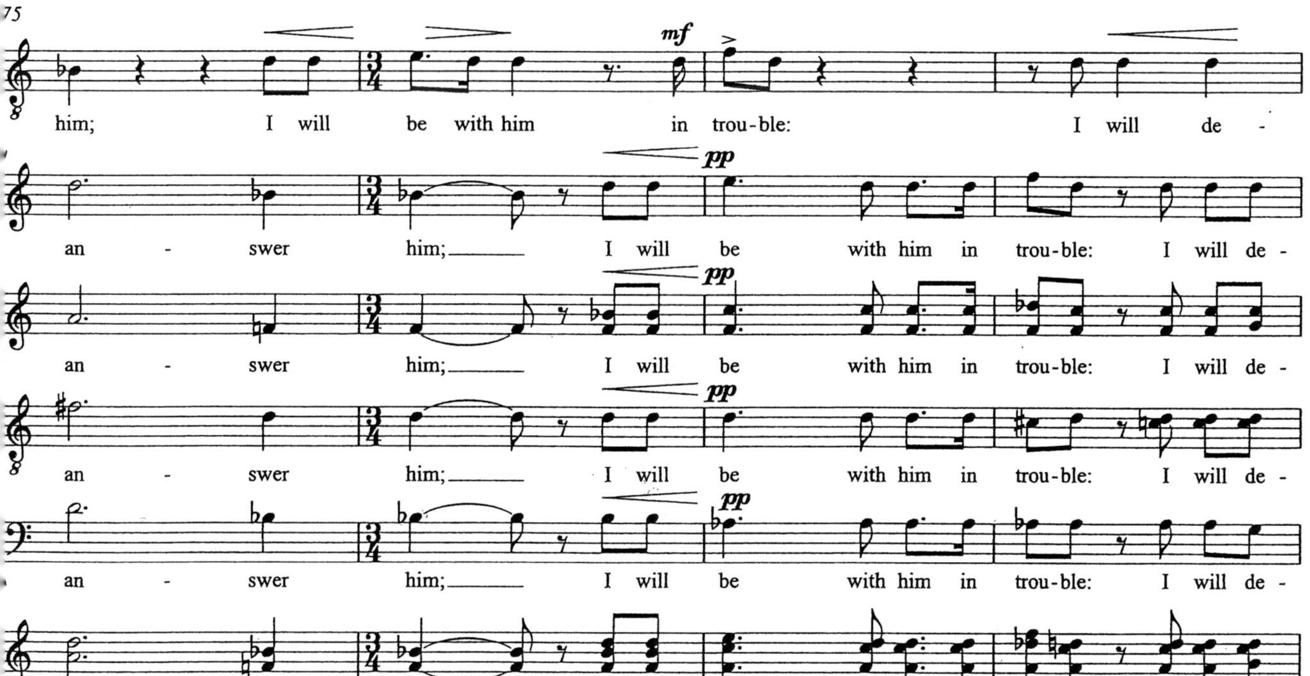
75
mf
him; I will be with him in trou - ble: I will de -
pp
an - swer him; I will be with him in trou - ble: I will de -
an - swer him; I will be with him in trou - ble: I will de -
an - swer him; I will be with him in trou - ble: I will de -
an - swer him; I will be with him in trou - ble: I will de -
pp

79
espr.
li - ver him, and hon - our him; With long life will I
pp sempre
long life will I
li - ver him, and hon - our him; With long life will I
pp sempre
li - ver him, and hon - our him; With long life will I
pp sempre
li - ver him, and hon - our him; With long life will I
pp sempre
li - ver him, and hon - our him; With long life will I
pp sempre

82
p
pp
sa - tis-fy him, and show him my sal - va - - - - tion.
and
ppp unis.
ppp
sa - tis - fy him, and show him my sal - va - tion.
ppp
ppp
will I sa - tis - fy him, and show him my sal - va - tion.
ppp
ppp
sa - tis - fy him, and show him my sal - va - tion.
ppp
ppp
sa - tis - fy him, and show him my sal - va - tion.
ppp

THE COMPLETE CHORAL MUSIC OF REBECCA CLARKE
AVAILABLE FROM OXFORD UNIVERSITY PRESS

Ave Maria
Unaccompanied Upper Voices (SSA)
0-19-386080-5

Chorus from Shelley's 'Hellas'
Unaccompanied Five-part
Women's Chorus (SSSAA)
0-19-386190-9

Come, Oh Come, My Life's Delight
Unaccompanied Mixed Chorus (SATB)
0-19-386660-9

He That Dwelleth in the
Secret Place of the Most High
Unaccompanied Mixed Choir (SSAATTBB)
with Solos (SAATB)
0-19-386661-7

A Lover's Dirge
Unaccompanied Mixed Chorus (SATB)
0-19-386665-X

Music, When Soft Voices Die
Unaccompanied Mixed Chorus (SATB)
0-19-386666-8

My Spirit Like a Charmed Bark Doth Float
Unaccompanied Mixed Chorus (SATB)
0-19-386667-6

Now Fie on Love
Unaccompanied Lower Voices (TTBarB)
0-19-386662-5

Philomela
Unaccompanied Mixed Chorus (SATB)
0-19-386663-3

There Is No Rose
Unaccompanied Lower Voices
(Solo Baritone, ATBarB Chorus)
0-19-386664-1

Weep You No More, Sad Fountains
Unaccompanied Mixed Chorus (SATB)
0-19-386668-4

When Cats Run Home and Light Is Come
Unaccompanied Mixed Chorus (SATB)
0-19-386669-2

10575

ISBN 0-19-386661-7

9 780193 866614